THE
elegance
OF ROOKS

THE
elegance
OF ROOKS

Jan Bay-Petersen

Osmanthus Publishing

Published by Osmanthus Publishing

First published 2024
© Copyright: Jan Bay-Petersen

Printed by imprintdigital
Upton Pyne, Exeter
imprintdigital.com

Typesetting and cover design by The Book Typesetters
hello@thebooktypesetters.com
07422 598 168
thebooktypesetters.com

ISBN 978-1-3999-9001-1

Acknowledgements

A number of these poems have been published in the following poetry journals; *Artemis, Stand, The Alchemy Spoon, The Interpreter's House, The North.* "Spellbinding for Bike" was shortlisted for the Plough Prize and published by *The Rialto*, "Owner of an Emptiness" won the 2013 Poetry Society Stanza Prize.

for Ole

Contents

The Elegance of Rooks

They perch around the walnut tree near the crossing.
This autumn, they have begun to stuff nuts
beneath the tyres of waiting cars.

They haven't mastered red lights yet,
the lethal tension between greed and green.
They hover, tentative and quick to squawk.

Like diplomats in a hard posting
rooks are inured to uproar;
if they lose their sangfroid it is on purpose.

Fluttered by dogs, they take off almost late,
flap low above those frantic, furry heads,
lure them out into the traffic.

Their bossy stride, like bellied aldermen, late
for an important meeting, can suddenly morph
into a balletic leap.

Those strong beaks, skilled at cracking skulls
of baby squirrels, disembowelling
crisp packets and fledglings

tenderly neck and nibble their own
as a soldier might gently stroke his baby
with a bayonet.

We respect their bravado, their lack of deference.
They are court jesters, barely tolerated,
we are their meat-in-waiting.

Kea[*]

They gaze at us
with bright remorseless eyes.

They fly to roadworks and shift traffic cones
inspect the halted cars,
remove windscreen wipers, hubcaps
with the accelerated grace
of a Formula One pit team.

Olive green, they blend
with miles of scree and wind-tormented scrub
until they fly –
the flash of underwings
the blaze of red.

At dawn in alpine tramping huts
glissando shrieks, a knifeblade scraping tin;
kea skiing down the roof
balanced on outstretched claws,
tumbling from gutters
raucous with delight.

Their mates eviscerate
rucksacks left unattended;
spread dirty laundry on display
puncture packs of food and mobile phones
stab tins and use them for lacrosse
hurl them from beak to beak.

Boots unlaced, their laces disappeared,
the ground peppered with eyelets.

After sparse forage for a million years
now kea gorge – potato crisps,
panini plucked from tourists,
kidney fat from living sheep.

Birds exist in the spaces between human lives,
once wide as the world.
The Southern Alps today are mined
by corridors of cars, that buffet kea,
press them flat; dried specimens
for a museum cabinet.

* Kea: Rhymes with "fear". The world's only alpine parrot, an endangered species native to New Zealand.

In a Southern Beech Forest[*]

In the north, beeches follow seasons. Here,
the great trees shed their leaves
slowly, as they are spent, throughout the year.
Even if I were lost and blind, I'd know
this smell of home: wet ferns
growing from a million years of mould.
Air rinsed by empty sea, no trace of smoke.

I'd find by ear a stream that flows from snow,
dip my hand, the numb ache in my bones,
drink the water that tastes of tumbled stones.
With luck, if it were spring and dawn was close
bellbirds would call, one silver chime answering another.
But so few left. There's nothing in this wood
that wouldn't thrive if we were gone for good.

[*] The Southern Beech of New Zealand, *Nothofagus* spp.
resembles the European beech but is evergreen.

Legacy

Driving slowly, steering with the skid
of gravel to an old house down a track.
The windscreen, the grasses near the ditch
the map beside me flapping on the seat,
all bear the same grey bloom. The garden's gone,
its boundary marked by brambles and a cattle grid.

The gutter swings, the roof is sway-backed,
peeling tin. The small squares on the map
showing the place which once held all we loved
is neat, precise; the contours follow close
around the hill. Lines scrawled with angry hands
show what is claimed and those who want it most.

Below, a metal sea. The tide is on the turn,
seabirds fret the line of clotted foam
where two strong currents meet. Too far
for any sound to reach the land, the gannets
stab the waves. We ache to wound
those faces that are too much like our own.

The Otago Goldfields

Tussock country
above the tree line
where there is stone
but no wood
they built hearths
without fires
except a flare
of grass stalks.

Water, but no tea.
Glacier water
tumbled with stones.
Stone flour but no bread.
The only shop a shack
ten miles' walk away
selling rum, beans,
biscuit, salt.

Payment in gold,
four grains to the carat,
two carats for a peck of beans.

Drystone huts
with no windows,
walls stunted to carry
thatch without rafters.
The only houses
built in this place
a string of kennels
threaded on rivers.

Winds from the ice cap
snow lying months on the tussock
all year on the peaks.
Fingers combed meltwater
panning for brightness
that would nestle in purses,
dance on the pulse
of a gleaming wrist.

Driving Through Floods, Northland, New Zeland

A shoreless lake, no settlement in sight.
Our convoy surges through in bottom gear
as ripples smack wet kisses on the doors.
The car ahead buffets with its bow wave

scours the mudguards with an amber wash.
The carpet bubbles beneath my feet.
I'm straining to get close and keep my distance
like someone wooing an indifferent lover.

Cars behind me overtake and pull away.
I am the last bead in a breaking string,
the road is somewhere underneath
between two lines of fencing.

No-one in sight. Fence-posts are squat.
Half-deleted trees stretch out like arms.
My car's a porous metal box
that lets in water, may not let me out.

No hurrying can make the journey shorter
no chance of turning back. As in illness
or growing old, success means getting through
the next small span of time.

To have a destination, a haven
where we might someday arrive, was a luxury
allowed when we were safe. For now, it is enough
that we maintain momentum, stay alive.

Owner of an Emptiness

I am smooth, delicate, enclosed.
A mere sigh would ruffle my composure

but I live deep, where no breath falls.
Darkness is nothing to me, moisture is all.

I am forced to gulp the falling bucket, but deflect
the blaze of blue, the hands, the cameo head.

Once a child fell in. Vainglorious on the rim,
terrified in his fall. I drank deep of him.

There is less of me than there was. Every day, the pail
takes longer to fall, and longer still to fill.

Last week a cat tied to a heavy stone
was dropped in by a woman who loathes

this place, the man who dragged her here.
I begin to stink, brilliantly.

The nights have been restless with the bleats
of children, their mothers, thirsty goats.

When I cease to be a well
all of them will cease to be.

Madame Cobra

Cobra Mist was the codename for an Anglo-American radar station at Orford Ness on the Suffolk coast, designed to give early warning of long-range missiles. Built in the 1960s, it suffered from mysterious noise interference and was closed down in 1973.

In a soft wind, the fabric round her flanks is silky
like a child's hair. In a soft light, her features blurred,
she is almost splendid, bulky against the sky,
an ageing actress watchful of the cameras.

Once she was protected, access controlled, photographed
only by permission. Now she lies open,
guardians and reason gone. Once painted to perfection,
now she's disheveled, hearing aids dangling loose

about her shoulders. For years she's been trying to ignore
the frazzled hiss and buzz of tinnitus,
straining to hear her cues above a flow
of sounds that never stop and don't exist.

Bleakly she awaits attention,
hoping to resume life in some new dramatic role,
forgetting that public tastes have changed
and her performance never quite came up to scratch.

Bletchley

He built intricate machines that smelled of sparks,
ticked as they decrypted deadly messages,
tended with tweezers by tired Wrens in the dark.

He was billeted with strangers; their boy in battledress
stared down from the sideboard. Every evening
he sat alone, the unknown, uninvited guest.

Terrified of talking in his sleep, he retreated
into crushing dreams that smelled of bitter almond.
Every day, jostled on a wooden seat

he rode a crowded bus that showed no name,
its headlights masked, to shabby wooden huts,
an ornate house, machine guns at the gate.

Relaxing with square roots of negatives,
quiet as a leveret crouched in its form,
he liked coins with prime dates, 1931 a favourite.

He kept custody of tongue like any monk; years later
he still searched for coded messages in number plates.

Pontcysyllte

Crossing Pontcysyllte, the glances of our helmsman
flicker from his careful course, sideways
and down to where blackbirds skim

through momentary shade between the arches,
down to where a hundred feet below
the river makes its own decisions.

Nineteen stone piers tapering like bluebell stalks
bearing iron arches cast at Plas Kyneston,
each dovetailed to its neighbour.

Eighteen curves like open wings.

Perhaps it comforts us to see a burden lightly borne
cathedral vaulting, canopies in leaf;
these arches lift four hundred thousand gallons

within a cast-iron trough a thousand feet in length
and only inches wider than the painted narrowboats
that glide in ordered lines above the Dee.

Telford's own recipe for caulking,
Welsh flannel dipped in boiling sugar,
the joints then sealed with lead.

Dry ever since.

No-one had a better eye than Telford for the lie of land.
His navigators dug out cuttings, used the soil
to raise embankments. And here, climbed high

with stones that they had shaped and squared by hand
with limestone mortar mixed with oxblood, iron,
to raise this quieter, straighter waterway.

But even as the aqueduct was opened
with a fifteen gun salute, Trevethick's locomotive,
a boiler set on wheels, was building up a head of steam.

Parallel steel rails, not waterways,
would link the nation's towns.
This lovely artefact is a dead end,

a journey going nowhere.

Audacity

For Alexander McQueen[*]

A blatancy of surplus – bugle beads,
gold filigree, Swarovski crystals,
pheasant feathers, foxes' fur and bones;
bright bloomers, rounded over buttocks
like low-slung pollen sacs on bees.

The simple grace
of hats without a crown
the brim a perfect circle.

High platform soles. Elegant dressage
through pools of shallow water,
like sandals worn by geishas
who are so valued, so protected
that others do their walking.

Women of rich men need beauty
and either money or a clever mouth.
His commentary:
black leather masks
tight over nose and eyes.

For the lips, an open zip.

Tapestry and tartan, the braided twill
of military uniforms.
Swanskin, the gleaming plumage
plucked, reset, to lie as smooth
on the living girl
as on the dead swan.

The oily crimson mouths.

Grooms in large churches
awaiting organ chords and brides
draped in grey expensive cobwebs
heads poised beneath
a high headdress of antlers.

* Inspired by *Savage Beauty*, the 2015 exhibition of Alexander McQueen's work at the V&A.

The Casino at Baden-Baden

A faint vinegar smell
of panic, merged with two hundred years
of pomade, perfumes,
cigars, assorted alcohols.

By daylight, the velvet curtains
are faded at the fringes,
the gilding on chairs, around mirrors,
slightly hazed;

the carpet woven with the city's coat of arms,
(endlessly repeated) is slightly worn
where heels have walked, jittered –
around the roulette wheels,

the blackjack, poker tables,
between the brace of heavy doors
that those entitled to go through
expect others to hold open.

We understand this is a décor
of the night – candles, chandeliers,
red and gold, the glint of jewels,
offset by darkness.

An oval bar, redout
for a pyramid of polished bottles;
at the apex, magnums
of Grey Goose vodka.

Shoulder to bulky shoulder
in a back room without chairs,
with a looser dress code,
the slot machines.

Coloured chips ticking off
the red, the black, the odd,
the even, allocating
what you own, what you'll ever earn.

Chances are the same
for every player, rich or poor,
but once the money's gone
Nicht geht's mehr.*

Light as dust motes, the memory
of losses of the past: pensions,
great estates, dowries of girls
who had hoped to marry.

Leaving through the unmarked exit
feels like failure: we have forfeited
a fortune that was waiting for us
hidden between two cards.

**Nicht geht's mehr*: Les jeux sont faits, no more bets.

A Citizen of Delft

In taverns, he drank with tinsmiths, coopers,
confectioners and wainwrights. He too was an artisan,
making slow squares of costly colour.
His wife grumbled at the price of pigments.
Lapis lazuli alone was worth
its weight in silver: she wondered
if a red skirt might have looked as well,
why he squandered the precious stuff as underpaint.

They both knew
that unless the coins flowed in, the colours died.

He painted on commission. Each image sought a patron
to become a painting – those empty chairs, those servants
pouring milk, rolling up their stockings, choosing fish.
The money burghers paid to buy a picture
cost them their safeguard against a shipwrecked cargo,
the falling price of peppercorns. Their wives
could not afford the new, enticing silks,
their children's shoes were patched, they ate less meat.

Why were they willing to pay so much
for a domestic portrait of a stranger?

Maybe they craved a keyhole glimpse –
through brick walls barely older
than themselves, through courtyards
and curtains leaking shadows –
of their neighbour's private version of being human,
a check against their own secluded lives
in this orderly small Dutch river town
which held all the people they had ever known.

Performance

After John Cage

First night at the Barbican. Silence falls
as the conductor lifts his baton. And continues.
A thousand waiting ears listen alert
their owners quiet and still. The orchestra sits grim
skilled hands gripping polished instruments,
all tuned, all mute. There are three parts:
a symphony of silence, a three-piece suite of smoke.
By the second movement, expectation foiled,
the audience turns sour. It coughs.
Eyes slide away from the conductor
and stare at polished shoes.
They clap, though, at the end.

When they performed this work in China
by the end of the first movement
there were mutterings. Complaints grew louder.
The third Tacet was marked by catcalls
and cheerful insults to the lazy orchestra.
Old men cracked melon seeds between their teeth.
The bag passed from hand to hand
a crackle of percussion in its wake.
Their seats had cost a lot. They'd paid for music.
Four minutes 33
was barely long enough to show
just who this space belonged to.

Off Track

Local people shrugged
looked past our ears
refused to tell us
if the old logging train still ran.
They resist tourists
as they once fought Japanese
who invaded these high ranges
to cut cedars.

Past bamboos in close columns
above a sea of clouds
we walked beside the rusting tracks.
We crossed space
on rotting wooden viaducts,
kicked pebbles that fell
past open wings of birds,
dropped soundless onto scree.

We came to a tunnel
gouged through granite,
a foot wider than the rails.
We went in. No torch.
Water dripping from an unseen roof.
We stumbled on, then tiny, distant,
a white porthole of light.
We stopped. It grew.

When adventure changes
from something that you do
to something done to you
it shatters into panic.
We ran back, slipping, bruised,
the engine slamming at our heels
like a bull that reached the gate
just as we swung to safety.

A Travelling Court of the Lords of Poverty

Our mission, to feed the hungry.
I remember their polite averted faces.

We exchanged name-cards at the buffet breakfast
then the air-conditioned bus
the ride past bamboo huts and scrubby hills
on barely metalled roads.

At the experimental field, hundreds waiting
led by the mayor, immaculate
in shoes like ours; the crowd barefoot
or in sandals cut from rubber tyres.
We sat beneath our canopy for speeches
they stood quietly in the sun.

We admired the maize, taller
than ourselves, the leafy emerald swords,
the fat gleaming kernels
that we'd helped breed.
They listened as we promised them
a better future in a foreign language.

The driver fossicked in the bus
brought out our lunches
a cardboard box of rice, topped
with a breaded cutlet, pickles.
A lunch for all the visitors
one extra for the mayor.

They didn't seem to grasp
that it was time for them to leave,

waited in silence as we ate.

Field Trip after the Conference, South Korea

We gather in good time beside the bus.
Those of us who struggle with our luggage
envy those with less. General admiration
for the lady from Mongolia, who has packed
her formal clothes of knee-high leather boots
and two silk quilted tunics, plus essentials,
into a small attaché case. Ready to start.
Our hosts count us three times.
The Englishman is late. Through the hotel window
we see him eating breakfast, peacefully.

At last we're all on board. Yesterday was rural banks,
today it's monuments. Our first stop:
a Buddhist temple on a peak, carried like a palaquin
on massive gilded beams. Laquered pillars,
roof of curving tiles. Our hosts inform us
that older temples on this site were burned,
three by the Japanese, two in wars with China.
We stand beaming in a group for photographs.
Everyone has noticed, no-one comments,
that the Englishman has wandered off alone.

Three Weeks After the Earthquake

We no longer consult the sky.
The weather that concerns us
is beneath our feet, our soles alert
for shudders, the first twitching.

Aftershocks feel like vertigo
or being drunk, then the crash
of everything still left to fall
tells us it is the earth reeling.

Buildings lurch to keep in step
movement heard as much as felt
Aolian harps of rebar vibrate,
strain, encased in tons of concrete.

We thought to help by clearing bricks
a line of helpers, hand to hand,
but stood helpless and silent
before tangles of steel knitting

endless strands thicker than our wrists
immoveable giant hawsers
mooring tilted concrete slabs,
deep strata, geological.

Each day for these last three weeks
they have been dying in the dark,
blood drying on their wounds, thirsty
and alone. We cannot find them

or we come too late –
we can only bury them again
this time in coffins, washed and dressed,
escorted by priests to mass graves.

We have lost our way
alleys are dead ends
highways are fissures
to the underworld.

One thing we know for sure –
our trust in solid earth was a mistake.
We know now just where we stand
how thin it is, provisional.

An Airborne Infection

Each morning outside the office door
a clerk records our temperatures.
We wait in line and eavesdrop
on each others' numbers,
reassure our colleagues
if they're higher than the day before.

The first symptoms
are a dry cough and fever.

Guardians with thermometers
stand at the doors of supermarkets, banks.
To stay free, we must keep our bodies cooler
than thirty-eight degrees.
We lose our taste for spicy food, move slowly,
ice our drinks and linger in the shade.

We are embarrassed by the doctors
who leapt from the ground floor windows
of the city hospital
just as they sealed the doors.
They showed the distance between ourselves
and the heroes we needed them to be.

Those locked inside
threw messages in plastic bottles.

We dread the breath of others;
wear face-masks in the street,
postpone haircuts and the dentist's chair
indefinitely. A current joke:
The quickest way to die from it –
cough in a crowded lift.

Shops long ago sold all their stocks
of disinfectant, bleach, thermometers
(jammed into our earholes like antennae).
A stall has prophylactic T-shirts.
They look like ordinary T-shirts
but sell out anyway.

We kiss our loved ones when they're leaving home
but not when they return.

There are brisk sales of broccoli, dried orange peel,
said to be effective against fever.
A neighbour uses all his disinfectant
to wash the seesaws in the playground,
protecting small children
he has never met.

We go alone at dawn or late at night
to pray for mercy
in churches and temples
fogged by incense.
Each of us has private, secret magic –
icons, whisky sours, aubergines.

The mastheads of the daily papers
show the death toll, printed in red.

Our Chinese Bed

Strangers in a strange land, groping to fit
our old selves into unknown spaces,
we clung to rules that still applied.
Firm beds build straight backs
helped us sleep in our Chinese bed –
a square-cut palliasse stuffed tight
with rice straw, covered by a finely woven mat.
In summer its patterned squares, diamonds
were stamped onto our skin, which sweated
where we touched the mat, each other.

Now, in a cold house in a colder country,
once familiar, we still sleep hard, stiff
as tomb effigies, awakening
with bruised hips and aching knees.
Once again, we are lopping off
what doesn't fit: the staccato plainsong
of a tonal language, dressing in colours
that acknowledge the occasion, the gentle use
of elbows to gain a place, moving through streets
as shoal fish do, or members of a murmuration.

A Life Ago

Even the fierce staff nurse is reverent, brings a screen
before she lavishes with suds the clear skin of his back
rubs it with alcohol, massages with zinc cream.
We student nurses, awed at having leave to touch,
grip hands beneath his slack, smooth body, heave.
We pull his bed-sheet taut so it won't chafe
then comb his glossy hair, adjust the thin
tube of his catheter, change his unused carafe.

The summer breeze brings to his still head
the breath of mown lawns, the smell of tar
from heat-hazed roads shimmering ahead
of fences flicking like eyelashes, immeasurably far
from this young man, ten miles and two months on
from the biker who rode wheelies, did the ton.

Nocturne

She hears a blackbird whistling to the spring
that's still three months away. The notes rebound
off ice, the boughs are bare, the grubs deep underground.
Fragile automata, the other birds begin to sing.
Black night, no eastern silhouette of dawn,
yet still the blackbird calls, willing the world
to warm, urging torpid birds to mate and build
their nests too early, breed oblivion.

The man who sleeps beside her moves through dreams
where she's a stranger: behind closed doors she senses
the murmur of his phone calls, and he seems
preoccupied, smells different: musky, sweet.
The cruellest lies are sometimes told in silence.
The birdsong swells like surf. She tries to sleep.

Final Movement

For Ann Johnson

Trees in autumn burn the sugars
of the summer: what grew slowly
over days of sunlight
flares brightly at the last.

So you bring to your end
virtues grown when you were strong:
courage that comes from walking
many miles alone in mountains
on faint trace of paths;
endurance born of travelling
tired, as far as strength could reach
in search of wonders.

Dear, may you go safe home,
knowing that in your fall
you leave the earth richer,
fed by your brilliant leaves.

Remembrance

On the long flight home, I read
the Tibetan Book of the Dead
the closest I could find to a gazeteer
showing where you'd gone, where to go from here.

The funeral as familiar as an old bruise,
maybe from movies. The vicar and his prayers,
the wreaths, the half-remembered family faces
your glossy coffin on its dais.

As I watched you sinking slowly underground
I strained to hear your spirit, but what came to mind
was something I hadn't realized that I knew:
All my life I've been afraid of you.

Fall

Oaks hold their colour till the limes are bare.
Our words lose shape, like raindrops on a stone.
We hear the slack feet fumbling on the stair.

We misremember poets who once sang here
then quietly left to face the night alone.
Oaks hold their colour till the limes are bare.

Age is another country, alien, where
we live without a passport, skulk at home,
hearing the slack feet fumble on the stair.

There is a kind of rest in it, aware
we only lease what once we thought to own.
Oaks hold their colour till the limes are bare.

Sleep's a mirage that fades as we draw near,
night featureless, the dawn in monochrome,
hearing the slack feet fumbling on the stair.

Once, years accrued like pearls; now we must bear
their compound weight, like necklaces of stone.
Oaks hold their colour till the limes are bare.
I hear the slack feet fumble on the stair.

Cyclamen

Even in still air
its backswept petals
call to mind a wind tunnel.
The leaves are elegant,
neat as a French beret
on a well-coiffed head.

Its habits are ascetic;
it prefers a hard bed
in mountains, of clay
packed as tight with pebbles
as billiard balls in a rack,
a rosary in a clenched fist.

Offered as a tribute,
it is not for marriages or love affairs;
it is a flower for funerals
or departures with long separations.
All parts are toxic.
It induces birth in pregnant women
who step over it
whether the baby is ready or not.

We take our revenge,
cramming potlets of damp peat
into sunless battery farms,
raising plants whose bright flowers
always fail to achieve
their destiny as seed
in the short space
between ripeness and rot.

Gravemates

Somewhere there lives a person who shall lie
next to me forever, each in our own small plot,
neighbours in an empty street of terraced houses
sharing the same postcode, our front doors side by side.

Living, we build our webs with care - who sits
at the twin schoolroom desk, who joins our gang,
who'll be our mate, our closest friend,
who'll dye and cut our hair or drill our teeth.

But at this last liaison, roughly sorted
by religion we lie flank
by random flank, with less modesty
than in the changing rooms of public baths.

For now, me and my gravemates live apart
unable to identify each other,
our separate wanderings like silver scribbles
left on a path when daylight dries the dew.

One day, drawn like nails to a magnet,
we shall come together, take up our tenancies.
I wonder where she is and what he's doing.
Our stones, what they will claim for us. The dates.

Doppelgangers

Humans who live alone slide into silence.
Our mouths move in rehearsal, then grow stiff
as if numbed by injections.

Versions of ourselves have love affairs
with characters on screens. We polish our profiles,
check anxiously in mirrors that we're real

confirm the details by confiding them, endlessly
to any listener, even one who isn't there.
What we ate. What we bought. Where we ache.

*

Details of our other selves grow sharper
if we live alone for months on end
in those rare, remote places without people.

After some time and unsurprised we see ourselves
in duplicate, distant or on the far side of a stream
busy with something that we can't distinguish;

never looking over to make contact
never getting close enough to touch
or hear what we are trying to say.

*

Doppelgangers wait nearby, invisible
for when we lose our dowry of companionship
in empty bottles, wildernesses, age.

Our minds make them out of yearning
for an intimate, but they stay aloof.
It feels as if they make themselves.

There's no harm in them. They have no secrets,
they know only what we know. The fear is who is recognized
when one of us walks out into the street.

Metaphors

Attempts to trap them end in their death
crushed in a powdery hand
or pinned on boards, rigid, their colours fading.
The thousand lenses of their compound eyes
see everyway at once, in colours
that differ from the ones we see.

Some try to tame them, develop skills
in the gentle netting of intangibles.
Others hunt them avidly as food.
V-shaped notches in their wings
mark survivors still flying free,
the almost-misses of a beak.

If we search for them
we'll find the places they like best
are not like ours. They are connoisseurs
of long winds, gusts and breezes,
are sometimes found clustered on dung
sipping salts with elegant scrolled tongues.

Occasionally one lands and clings
with tiny, stinging feet.
Loathe to brush it off, we stand immobile,
locked in stasis until it wants to move
though we long to swat it
with a dictionary.

They are best spotted slantwise
by sideways vision vigilant for movement.
We may gaze, perhaps take notes,
what colours border where on the bright wings,
those hasty scribbles all we have to keep
when they take flight, which is always soon.

May on the M1

Up in Yorkshire buds are black,
barely break the bark; driving south,
spines are adorned with pearls,
then frothy sprays, constellations;

near Watford Gap petals drift
onto the tarmac, pointillé dots
of green; at Staples Corner
the vivid spoon-shaped leaves.

Late winter to mid-spring
in two hundred minutes
along a double corridor of scrub
severed by interchanges

both rows responding
to the nudging of heat, light
in a faultless Mexican wave
two hundred miles long

precise as the ripple
of a snare drum tattoo
each bush resolute
in its tempo

amidst the gassy puffs
of truck exhausts, the heat shimmer
over bonnets, the flash
of orange warning lights.

Like the slow spread of foam
edging a breaking wave,
blackthorn along the verge
bush by bush comes into bloom.

Survivor, September

Generous with gold as a brass band in sunshine;

Inscribed leaves lobed like flippers of Permian amphibians,

Neighbours now extinct. Overnight they fall

Kissing her feet, illuminating the autumn grass,

Gilding the ground. Forebears of dinosaurs ate her fruit,

Oval, soft and stinking. Hundred-million-year-old eggs.

Bugloss

It grows on sandy chalk, where grass
is meagre and burnt brown in summer.
If you fossick among the prickly ox-tongue
leaves, you will leave beads of blood.
If you dig down through its strong, dry roots
deeper than any dog ever dug
you will come to the end of the soil
before you come to the end of bugloss roots.

Don't be fooled by the flowers.
The soil in bugloss country is rich in seeds.
By the time you see the first small leaf
the root is longer than your foot.
Gardens abandoned for a month
convert, fervently, to bugloss.
Colonies flourish in new-found lands
behind bus shelters and bins.

Sometimes a hiss of herbicide
announces workmen with their sprayers.
Soon the plants are withered, fuse
into a dark brown crust. It doesn't feel like triumph.
We know that under the dead leaves
the roots are clenching their fingers
deeper in the chalk, honing survival skills
already older, more resilient than ours.

What the Dinosaurs Became

Having lost their mastery of earth
they have retreated into water
or into air, where lightweight,
their bones have been whittled
into latticework. Homeless, they find sleep
on any perch they can reach.

For just a few weeks each year
they build citadels – a goblet
of spittle-softened clay, a grassy nest
braced with inadvertent plastic –
to protect, not their fragile selves
but the eggs they still lay.

They are still clothed in feathers,
have retained the warm blood,
the naked three-toed feet,
but have lost the sharp teeth
of their ancestors, have dwindled,
become food for mammals.

They defy their role as prey
with coloured plumage, vivid beaks;
proclaim themselves,
their whereabouts, at daybreak
fortissimo with fanfares,
loud arpeggios.

All living things transform through time,
adapting to the world as it is
and to what it is becoming.
Another sixty million years
will show what traits, if any,
can carry forward this ancient lineage –

perhaps the blind flightless probing
of the kiwi; or the reclusion of kingfishers,
bright barbs deep in burrows
above clear running water;
or the solitary flight of the albatross
aloft for years on end.

Planting up

They stand tossing tulip bulbs
pansies, primulas in patterns
over freshly furrowed
municipal beds. Like migrating birds
they are an event of spring and autumn
their dormant skill
triggered by some change
the rest of us don't see.

They begin at the outer rim
dropping plantlets at their feet
then precision work
as the pattern moves
towards the centre.
They have no diagram
do not consult each other
look only at the finely crumbled soil.

When they have finished
there are no empty spaces
and no surplus. They rest
a few minutes, then step forward
to hoe the planting holes,
lightly toe in the plants,
tread them firm, kickstart
mandalas of the summer.

Green Fingers

After David Hart

"A good man's place is underneath good earth."
– Yiddish Proverb

If the soul of my dead father remembers anything
he will remember the fertile strip of earth
around this house; he will note the health of trees,
the weight of fruitfall and the season's rain.

If he remembers anything, it will be the feel
of finely crumbled humus, the feral
tang of bonemeal. Soil on his tongue
could talk to him, of minerals and mould.

He knew it as a matrix through which matter
dances in a thousand living forms.
A good man's place is underneath good earth
while his bones course through the roots and bud the branches.

Flittermice

They fly with their fingertips,
skeletons like birdbone, wings
taut as drumskins,

calling as they navigate the dark,
relying not on answers
but on echoes:

the sharp vibrato of gnat wings, moths,
the breath of owl feathers. The muffled drum-roll
of beetle feet.

Their pitch is low when they chatter
with their fellows, raising the tone
when excited,

jostling each other without touch,
competing for food, to be owners
of the same space,

seeking mates. Males in autumn
crouch singing on chimney pots
eight-octave serenades

which we are deaf to. Their world is silence
until a device translates the frequencies
for human ears.

Pipistrelles, wet sheets slapping
on a rock; the squeaky ratchets
of water bats

floating over ponds like hovercraft;
the long-eared whispering bat
hunting on the wing

by sound alone, continuous chip-chop
like a thousand ultrasonic
chopsticks,

darting through woodland after moths
avoiding trees, twigs, a thread
of gossamer.

Bat Handlers

We do not need leashes, jesses or hoods.
They stay at their will or leave. They bite
but not deeply. An exaggerated nip,

almost a love bite. We accept their stigmata
as we consent to being regularly pierced
by injections of antirabies vaccine.

Those we fly range from the trusting,
almost confiding – winged hamsters –
to hermits, intent on holy quiet

the dark seclusion of inner caves.
They scramble to hide in our armpits
when threatened, shriek soundlessly

until a recorder with a microphone
translates their calls for human ears
and we hear their six-octave cadenzas

perfectly pitched, so acutely heard
that the echoes guide them at speed
through three dimensions.

We find the adults battered but alive
beside roads, wind turbines. If taken too young
they die for lack of batmilk.

Sometimes they arrive as older kits
that have crept curious out of lofts
onto disconcerted curtain rails.

They fly at night, prefer moonlight to human lamps,
have no party pieces. They may catch moths
flying above barbecues, but only if the guests

sit motionless and silent. Their mews
is a wardrobe where coats must hang
unused throughout the winter.

We are a deaf audience
in their world – a concert hall
where all are singers, virtuosi.

A Specimen of *Octopus vulgaris* in the New Zealand National Aquarium

They called him Inky. With time
he seemed to recognise
their individual torsos
so different from his own.
He signalled, watched them
with his large observant eyes.

Irredeemably rigid
they were unable to respond
to his eight fluent arms
owning more than half his brain,
each seeing, tasting,
moving independently.

The rest of the brain, a doughnut
round his throat, used for planning,
solving problems, memory –
of cold sand, the moving plane
where air and water meet
which Inky crossed with ease.

Octopuses love to play with net floats,
with lost revolving beach-balls,
to open jars and hide inside them.
They exit fish-traps as smoothly
as they enter them, leaving a litter
of fishbones, lobster shells.

From his covered tank
in an amphitheatre full of tanks
lit by neon lights, where molluscs
faithfully observe their own tides,
feeding, closing in rhythm
with the shores where they were captured

Inky raised the lid, climbed out,
clambered across the tiled floor
squeezed his bulbous head
and errant arms into an outflow pipe
two inches wide leading to the sea
and went home.

The scientists still check his tank
each morning when they come to work,
hoping he might return.

Wadden Sea, Friesland

Intertidal land between two seas,
marsh giving way to sediments

as fine as talc, but oozing
wet and flooded twice a day.

To reach knee depth
you need to wade a mile

wadlopen[*] through
deep mud and shallow water.

Heavy columns, we are the wrong shape
for this terrain; a false step

and we plummet like driven piles.
into the bed of the North Sea.

Better to wait quietly
until the tide comes in

sharing the endless shore
with scattered silhouettes of gulls

balanced on a meniscus
near the water's edge

above a second bird
mirrored in wet silt.

its water glaze
anchored to their feet

quick-stepping in unison
crab eggs, sea worms up into the light

printing brief, broad arrows that point
everywhere, around the dancing birds.

* *Wad*: Dutch for mud. *Wadlopen*: Mudhiking.

Harbour

If she concentrates, quiet and alone,
she can still see the contours of the beach
she and her brother regarded as their own

where after school they would haul
their canoe across the mud
to the gleaming ribbon of the tidal channel

and paddle to the islet edged
with honeycombed clay banks
where kingfishers nested;

a silent place, inhabited by reeds,
rats and birds, explored by paths
made by their own bare feet.

The shoreline has gone, the outline of the hills,
but she can still hear underfoot
the crunch of empty clam shells,

the scrape along the keel, the suck and slide
of their canoe riding like a sleigh
down the braidings of the ebb tide;

the sudden splash, once afloat,
the skittish flurry at the water's edge,
the welcome loss of weight;

the rare alien sun-dried
Portuguese Men O'War,
abandoned by the tide.

They would pick their careful way,
she and her brother, past clumped
sapphire stingers, skeins

of poisonous hackled flax
each with a thousand toxic stings,
the blue bladders of the air sacs.

At the far end of her lifetime, she still feels
the shock when they returned too late
to find a full tide, the jellyfish set free,

air floats sailing before the breeze,
each with twenty feet of tentacles
drifting invisible beneath.

Wading together to the empty shore, mid-shin
in the tawny, tepid water
which had ambushed them,

dragging the canoe through the shallows,
each gripping a gunwale, stoic,
probing the silt blindly with their toes;

then as now, she and her brother,
each knowing that the other was afraid,
that they could trust each other.

The Faith Healer of Cars

It was the kind of old car you talk to
when you're driving on your own
urging it on

your ears alert
for rattles, wheezes,
like the parent of a child with asthma.

It stopped dead on a roundabout
in the rush hour in the city centre,
jammed it solid

and that was when he came up
laid his hands upon the bonnet
and blessed it.

The car started of course, or this wouldn't be a story
and I waved and shouted thanks,
drove away

leaving behind the questions
I lacked the time to ask
or even think of.

Whether he was a mechanic
with psychic powers, diagnosing
engine failure,

mending faulty parts
without a need to touch them
or even see them,

or if the car
somehow recognised him,
spoke to him, and he replied;

something in the car
I didn't know was there,
calling out

to something in him
that most of us don't have
or know about;

which might make roadside garages
with their petrol pumps
almost like churches.

Spellbinding for Bike

Pluck a shoot of what grows fast
and fragile, weave it through the spokes –
scarlet runner, mile-a-minute.
Lick your finger, bless the brakes
so they grip firm but not too tight
when lights turn red on downward slopes
lest potholes, ruts, betray your wheels
on black ice, white ice, frozen snow.

Turn the back wheel widdershins
before you mount, burnish the bell
and ring it when you pass a church
or petrol station. Let the smell
of diesel serve as musk to mark
the beast, its metal jaws that chewed,
unraveled those who once were strong
and confident, as fast as you.

They now ride ghost bikes, painted white,
hung with funeral wreaths, and rags
of faded ribbons, photographs
and weeping notes in plastic bags.
May the gods grant you don't mistake
lycra for armour, or think that luck's
forefinger, crooked, guides your path.
It beckons to the cars. The trucks.

It's a Two and You're Dead

The closer we live to our gods, the more we need games.
Luck isn't random: it chooses and fondles, then flits,
while we phantom midges soar high on the breath
of the gods or are drowned in their spit.
If our buzzing offends, if we stick in their throat,
they may take as amends what we don't want to lose,
and we pay with an arm and a leg. Let us pray.

Playing games gives a hint. They're a rear-vision mirror
to show what is coming up close from behind.
They won't stop the truck, but maybe you'll pause
a significant tick while you're sending a text
so your paths don't collide. If you're ten over par,
if your darts hit the wire - give the blind date a miss.
Don't ask for a raise, not today. Catch the bus.

Wait till you throw double six, till your horse
gallops home, till the ball draws a line
from your boot to the goal, till the Queen, King and Knave
join the cloverleaf Ace. Though you can't read the stars
you can tip them like Braille and the rhythms are good,
your sails belly and fill, the duck's entrails are pink.
There's a cat and he's black and you're blessed. Take the trick.